Phonics and Reading Skills

This book belongs to

_____

For information regarding permission, write to:
Scholastic Education International (Singapore) Pte Ltd
81 Ubi Avenue 4, #02-28 UB.ONE, Singapore 408830
Email: education@scholastic.com.sg

For sales enquiries write to:

Latin America, Caribbean, Europe (except UK), Middle East and Africa
Scholastic International
557 Broadway, New York, NY 10012, USA
Email: intlschool@scholastic.com

Philippines
Scholastic Philippines
Penthouse 1, Prestige Tower, F. Ortigas Jr. Road,
Ortigas Center, Pasig City 1605
Email: educteam@scholastic.com.ph

Asia (excluding India and Philippines)
Scholastic Asia
Plaza First Nationwide, 161, Jalan Tun H S Lee,
50000 Kuala Lumpur, Wilayah Persekutuan Kuala Lumpur, Malaysia
Email: international@scholastic.com

Rest of the World
Scholastic Education International (Singapore) Pte Ltd
81 Ubi Avenue 4 #02-28 UB.ONE Singapore 408830
Email: education@scholastic.com.sg

Australia
Scholastic Australia Pty Ltd
PO Box 579, Gosford, NSW 2250
Email: scholastic_education@scholastic.com.au

New Zealand
Scholastic New Zealand Ltd
Private Bag 94407, Botany, Auckland 2163
Email: orders@scholastic.co.nz

India
Scholastic India Pvt. Ltd.
A-27, Ground Floor, Bharti Sigma Centre,
Infocity-1, Sector 34, Gurgaon (Haryana) 122001, India
Email: education@scholastic.co.in

Visit our website: www.scholastic.com.sg

First edition 2013
Reprinted 2014, 2015, 2017

ISBN 978-981-07-1359-1

Welcome to Learning Express!

Helping your child build essential skills is easy!

These teacher-approved activities have been specially developed to make learning both accessible and enjoyable. On each page, you'll find:

Focus Skill
The focus of each activity page is clearly indicated.

Instructions
The read-aloud instructions are easy for your child to understand.

Meaningful learning
Each activity has been carefully designed to make your child's learning meaningful and fun.

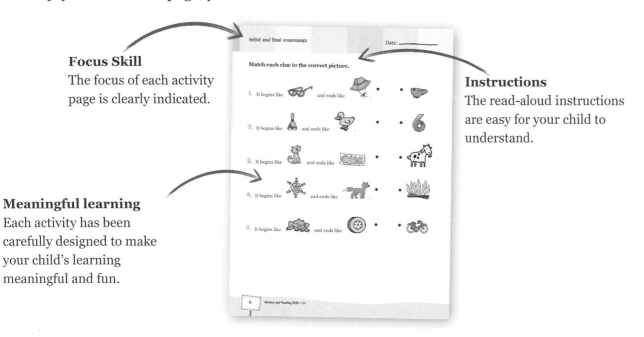

This book also contains:

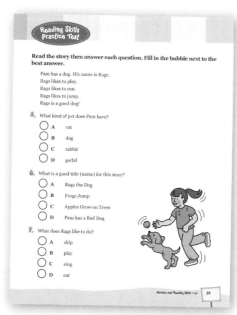

Instant assessment to ensure your child really masters the skills.

Completion certificate to celebrate your child's leap in learning.

Motivational stickers to mark the milestones of your child's learning path.

Contents

Phonics/Spelling

Understanding the relationship between letters and the sounds they make, or phonics, is a giant step in learning to read. A good grasp of phonics will help your child become better at spelling.

What to do

The activity pages in this section will give your child practice in identifying and spelling long- and short-vowel sounds, consonant blends, consonant digraphs and rhyming words.

Have your child complete the activities on each page. Review the work together. Praise your child for a job well done!

Keep On Going!

Play a phonics/spelling game with your child. Set up word clues and ask your child to say and spell the word. For example:

> I start with the *bl* sound.
> I have a short-*o* vowel.
> I end with the *k* sound
> I rhyme with stock.
> What word am I? (block)

Have your child give you clues so you can guess the word.

Date: _____

Match each clue to the correct picture.

1. It begins like and ends like .   ●   ●

2. It begins like and ends like .   ●   ●

3. It begins like  and ends like .   ●   ●

4. It begins like and ends like  .   ●   ●

5. It begins like and ends like .   ●   ●

Date: _____

Match each word at the bottom of the page to the word that has the same letters. Write the word in the box. Then write the letters that stand for the beginning and ending sound of each word. The first one has been done for you.

	Beginning Sound	Ending Sound

1. bus

   [sub]   b   s

        s   b

2. tip

   [   ]   ___   ___

        ___   ___

3. ten

   [   ]   ___   ___

        ___   ___

4. pal

   [   ]   ___   ___

        ___   ___

5. pot

   [   ]   ___   ___

        ___   ___

6. gas

   [   ]   ___   ___

        ___   ___

| top | net | sag | pit | lap | sub |

Date: _____

 X *makes the sound of* ks. *(Hint: Say the word* kiss *very fast!) Most of the time, an* **x** *is in the middle or at the end of a word.*

Help Superhero X put the missing x in each word. Then draw a line to the matching picture.

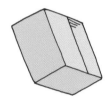

fo____

mi____er

ta____i

e____it

a____

si____

o____

bo____

e____ercise

tu____edo

Date: —————————

Sometimes a consonant may make no sound at all. For example, when k and n come together, the k is silent. When w and r come together, the w is silent. When r and h come together, the h is silent.

Look at the words and pictures. Draw a sleepy eye, like this: 〜〜 above the consonant that is silent. Do not color it. Then color the other letters in the word.

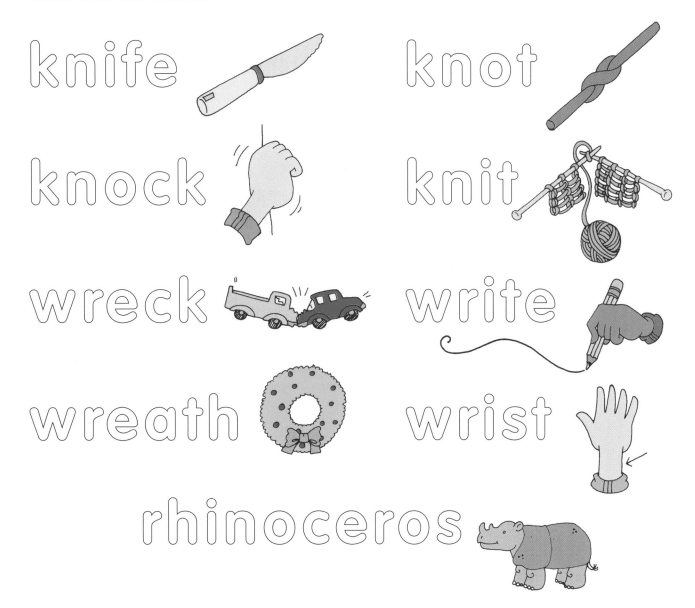

knife

knot

knock

knit

wreck

write

wreath

wrist

rhinoceros

Date: _____

Read to find out why these children got into trouble. Circle all the double consonants in each sentence. Then find the picture that goes with the sentence. Write the number of the sentence in the correct box.

1. Aki and Jamal giggled in class.

2. Emma and Jenna scribbled on the wall.

3. Hina and Kelly tattled to Mommy.

4. Dai and Kenny held a muddy puppy.

Date: _____

Make your own rhyming words. Look at the picture and say the word. Copy the word. Then change the first letter using each of the letters on the hammer to make new words.

p s r m f h b

h c m t w f

f j l h

s l b

ball

cat

dog

hand

Poems are made with rhyming words. Read the Mother Goose rhymes. Find a word from the box below to rhyme with each underlined word. Copy the word on the line.

1. Jack and <u>Jill</u>

   Went up the _____

   To fetch a pail of water.

   Jack fell <u>down</u>

   And broke his _____,

   And Jill came tumbling after.

2. Hey diddle <u>diddle</u>

   The cat and the _____,

   The cow jumped

   over the <u>moon</u>.

   The little dog laughed

   to see such sport,

   And the dish ran

   away with the _____.

3. Hickory dickory <u>dock</u>

   The mouse ran up the

   _____.

   The clock struck one,

   The mouse ran down

   Hickory dickory dock.

4. Mary had a little lamb,

   Its fleece was white

   as _____.

   Everywhere that Mary went,

   The lamb was sure to g<u>o</u>.

Word Box

fiddle	snow	crown	clock	hill	spoon

Date: _____

 Sp *makes the sound you hear at the beginning of the words* **Spike** *and* **spider**.

Spike the spider wants to catch sp words in his web. Color each picture that begins with sp. There are eight of them. Draw an X on the pictures that do not begin with sp.

 This begins with *sp*. It is a green vegetable. It is good for you. Popeye eats it to make him strong. What is it?

Date: _____

 Sn *makes the sound you hear at the beginning of the words* **Sniffles** *and* **snake**.

Why is Sniffles the snake crying? He is lost! Help him find his way back to his mother. First, color only the pictures that begin with sn. Then use those clues to draw the path to Sniffles' mother.

Sm *makes the sound you hear at the beginning of the words* **Smiley** *and* **Smith**.

Help Smiley Smith find the correct answers. He is looking for one picture in each row that begins with sm. Draw a smiley face in each box whose picture begins with sm.

 1.

2.

3.

Date: _____

St *makes the sound you hear at the beginning of the words* **Stella** *and* **stars**.

Stella has made up a game for you! Use the star code to make words that begin with st. Write the correct letter above each star. Then draw a line to match each word you made to the correct picture.

A   C   E   F   H   I   K   L   M   O   P   R   S   T   V

 1. ___ ___ ___ ___ ___

 2. ___ ___ ___ ___ ___

 3. ___ ___ ___ ___ ___ ___ ___

 4. ___ ___ ___ ___ ___ ___

 5. ___ ___ ___ ___ ___

 6. ___ ___ ___ ___ ___

Date: _____

 Tw *makes the sound you hear at the beginning of the words* **Twila** *and* **twins**.

Twila's twins love to ask questions. Read each question below. Find a word that answers the question and write it in the correct bubble.

Tweezers	Tweet! Tweet!	Twelve	Twirl!	Twister	Twenty

Str *makes the sound you hear at the beginning of the word* **strike**.

Look at the pictures on the baseball caps below. If the picture begins with str, make red stripes on the cap. If the picture does not begin with str, color the whole cap yellow.

Date: _____

*When two consonants come together and make one new sound, these consonant letters are called **digraphs**.*

Look at the man making new sounds in the digraph machine. He puts in two letters, but only one sound comes out!

Now you try it! Look at the two letters. When the word comes out at the end, draw a green circle around the two letters that make the new sound. That is the digraph!

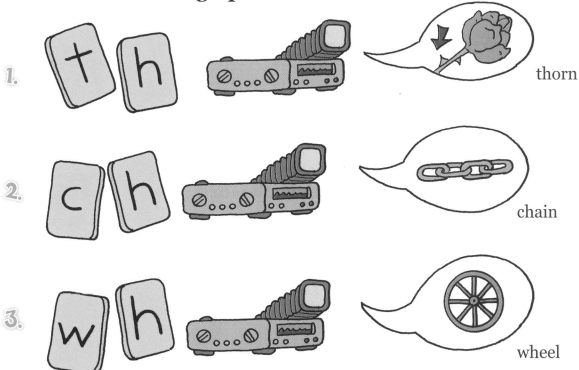

1. thorn

2. chain

3. wheel

The letters **th** *make the sound at the beginning of the word* **thorn**.

A. Read each list word. Circle the letters th in each word.

 Read.   **Copy.**   **Organize.**

list words that
begin with **th**

1. the   _____

2. this   _____   _____

3. with   _____   _____

4. then   _____   _____

5. bath   _____   _____

6. that   _____

 Challenge Words

list words that
end with **th**

7. them   _____   _____

8. they   _____   _____

B. Write the list word that rhymes with each word.

1. path _____   2. den _____   3. rat _____

Unscramble each list word.

4. het _____   5. hiwt _____   6. tsih _____

Date: _____

*The letters **sh** make the sound at the beginning of the word **shell**.*

A. Read each list word. Circle the letters sh in each word.

 Read.   **Copy.**    **Organize.**

		list words that begin with **sh**
1. ship	_____	
2. she	_____	_____
3. fish	_____	_____
4. shape	_____	_____
5. wish	_____	
6. brush	_____	list words that end with **sh**

 Challenge Words   _____

7. shine   _____   _____

8. shoe   _____   _____

B. Draw a  around the list word that is spelled correctly.

1. shipe   ship   2. shape   shap   3. she   shee

4. fish   fich   5. brosh   brush   6. wich   wish

Date: _____

*The letters **ch** make the sound at the beginning of the word **chain**.*
*The letters **wh** make the sound at the beginning of the word **wheel**.*

A. Read each list word. Circle the letters ch and wh in each word.

Read.

Copy.

Organize.

	Read.	Copy.	Organize.
1.	chin	_____	list words that begin with **ch**
2.	chop	_____	_____
3.	whale	_____	_____
4.	when	_____	list words that begin with **wh**
5.	inch	_____	_____
6.	which	_____	_____

Challenge Words
_____

7.	why	_____	list words that end with **ch**
8.	what	_____	_____

_____

B. Write the list word that rhymes with each word.

1. tail _____   2. mop _____   3. pinch _____

4. pitch _____   5. pen _____   6. win _____

Date: _____

*The letters **ck** make the sound at the end of the word **pick**.*

A. Read each list word. Circle the letters ck in each word.

 Read.   **Copy.**   **Organize.**

list words with short -a sound

1. duck _____

_____

2. pack _____

list words with short -e sound

3. stick _____

_____

4. back _____

list words with short -i sound

5. neck _____

_____

6. rock _____

list words with short -o sound

Challenge Words

_____

7. clock _____

list words with short -u sound

8. quick _____

_____

B. Write the list word that matches each picture.

1. _____ 2. _____ 3.  _____

4.  _____ 5.  _____ 6.  _____

*The letters **ar** make the sound at the beginning of the word **arch**.*

A. Read each list word. Circle the letters ar in each word.

 Read. **Copy.** **Organize.**

1. are   _____   list words with **ar** in the middle

2. hard   _____   _____

3. star   _____   _____

4. jar   _____   _____

5. part   _____   other list words

6. farm   _____   _____

🏆 Challenge Words
               _____

7. start   _____   _____

8. shark   _____   _____

B. Write the list word that rhymes with each word.

1. card _____   2. art _____   3. harm _____

4. car _____ *and* _____ *and* _____

Date: _____

*The letters **or** make the sound at the beginning of the word **ornament**.*

A. Read each list word. Circle the letters or in each word.

 Read.   **Copy.**   **Organize.**

1. or   _____   two- or three-letter list words

2. corn   _____   _____

3. porch   _____   _____

4. horn   _____   four- or five-letter list words

5. for   _____   _____

6. short   _____   _____

 Challenge Words   _____

7. your   _____   _____

8. horse   _____

B. Write the list word that begins with the same sound as each picture.

1. _____   2.  _____   3.  _____

4.  _____   5.  _____   6.  _____

Throughout the year, see if you can learn all the words in this spelling list.

an	do	if	or	tape
and	dog	inch	pack	ten
are	duck	is	park	that
arm	end	jar	part	the
as	farm	jump	play	then
at	feet	kite	porch	this
ate	fish	let	rain	thorn
back	fly	like	red	to
bath	for	love	rock	top
big	fork	make	rope	tray
black	fox	math	run	tree
bone	from	me	see	up
brush	gave	men	seed	wait
bug	get	mud	shape	we
but	go	my	she	whale
by	got	nail	ship	when
cake	had	name	shop	which
came	hand	neck	short	white
can	hard	need	sit	wish
car	hat	nine	six	with
chin	him	north	so	yes
chip	his	nose	star	you
chop	home	not	stay	
corn	hop	note	stick	
day	horn	of	sun	
dish	I	on	tail	

Fill in the bubble next to the correct answer.

1. Which word has the **silent k sound**?

    ◯ **A** knife

    ◯ **B** kite

    ◯ **C** kit

    ◯ **D** kind

2. Which word has the **silent w sound**?

    ◯ **A** wind

    ◯ **B** write

    ◯ **C** white

    ◯ **D** weak

3. Which word does not have a digraph sound?

    ◯ **A** chain

    ◯ **B** cap

    ◯ **C** thin

    ◯ **D** ship

Fill in the bubble next to the correct answer.

4. Which word rhymes with **love**?

   ○ **A** come

   ○ **B** from

   ○ **C** dove

   ○ **D** some

5. Which word rhymes with **high**?

   ○ **A** fright

   ○ **B** sight

   ○ **C** sigh

   ○ **D** night

6. Which word answers the following riddle?
   I shine in the sky. What am I?

   ○ **A** Mars

   ○ **B** star

   ○ **C** Earth

   ○ **D** Saturn

Fill in the bubble next to the correct answer.

7. Which word does not have a digraph sound?

  ○ **A**   fish

  ○ **B**   find

  ○ **C**   rack

  ○ **D**   whale

8. Which word rhymes with **kind**?

  ○ **A**   mine

  ○ **B**   find

  ○ **C**   fine

  ○ **D**   child

9. Which word rhymes with **start**?

  ○ **A**   lit

  ○ **B**   part

  ○ **C**   step

  ○ **D**   line

Fill in the bubble next to the correct answer.

10. Which word does not have the **sn consonant blend**?

⃝ **A**   star

⃝ **B**   snow

⃝ **C**   sneeze

⃝ **D**   snip

11. Which word has a **sm consonant blend**?

⃝ **A**   snail

⃝ **B**   smoke

⃝ **C**   ship

⃝ **D**   skip

12. Which word has a **tw consonant blend**?

⃝ **A**   thick

⃝ **B**   tip

⃝ **C**   twelve

⃝ **D**   sweet

Reading Skills

In this section, your child reviews previously learned reading skills and is introduced to new ones. These essential skills will help your child better comprehend what he or she is reading.

What to do
Read each page with your child. Then have him or her complete the activities. Be sure to review your child's work.

Keep On Going!
Have your child choose a book and read it together. Start by asking your child to look at the cover of the book. Have him or her predict what the story will be about based on the cover picture. Next, while reading, stop every few pages and ask questions. *Where did the story take place? Describe the main characters. What do you think will happen next? What problem does the main character face? How is the problem solved? Can you retell the story in your own words?* This process is called active reading. Good readers are active readers!

Date: _____

Tim is a good reader. He uses clues to help him read. First, he looks at the pictures. That helps him know what the story is about. Next, he reads the title of the story. Now he knows a little more. As he reads the story, the words make pictures in his mind.

Color in the book beside the correct answer.

1. Who is Tim?

 a good reader

 a math whiz

2. What does Tim do first?

 reads the story

 looks at the pictures

3. What else helps Tim know what the story will be about?

 the title

 the page number

4. As he reads, what makes pictures in Tim's mind?

 the letters

 the words

Date: _____

 The **main idea** *tells what the whole story is about.*

Today I went to the circus. My favorite part of the circus were the clowns. Clowns can do funny tricks. A clown named Pinky turned flips on the back of a horse. Fancy Pants juggled balls while he was singing a funny song. Happy Hal made balloons into animal shapes. Then twelve clowns squeezed into a tiny car and rode away.

Color in the ball that tells the main idea.

Pinky rides a horse.

Balloons can be shaped like animals.

Clowns can do funny tricks.

Clowns drive tiny cars.

Fancy Pants sang a song.

Date: _____

Trucks do important work. Dump trucks carry away sand and rocks. Cement trucks have a barrel that turns round and round. They deliver cement to workers who are making sidewalks. Fire trucks carry water hoses and firefighters. Oil is delivered in large tank trucks. Flatbed trucks carry wood to the people who are building houses.

Find the sentence in the story that tells the main idea. Write it in the circle below. Then draw a line from the main idea to all the trucks that were described in the story.

When you were born, your parents thought of a name for you. You might be named after someone in the family. Maybe you were named after a movie star! Almost every name has a meaning. Pamela means "honey." Henry means "master of the house." Ellen means "bright." Sometimes books about baby names tell the meanings. Many of the meanings will surprise you!

A. Circle the name below that has the main idea of the story in it.

B. To find out the meanings of the names in the puzzle below, follow each string of beads. Copy the letters on each bead in order in the boxes.

1. Casey means

2. Samir means

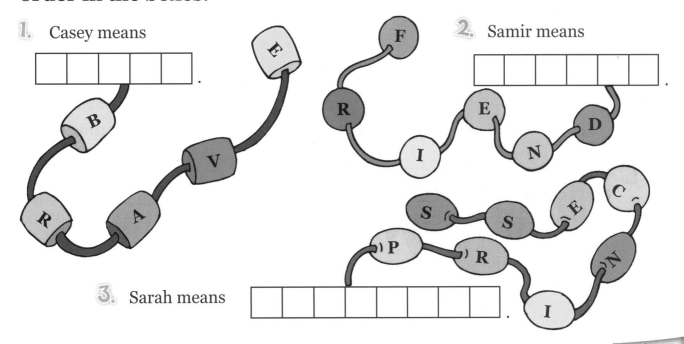

3. Sarah means

Date: _____

Details *are parts of a story. Details help you understand what the story is about.*

Skunks are small animals that live in the woods. They have black fur with one or two white stripes down their backs. Bugs are their favorite food. They also eat mice. If a skunk raises its tail, run away! Skunks can spray a very smelly liquid at anyone who bothers them.

Write the answers in the crossword puzzle.

Across

2. What color are the stripes on a skunk's fur?

5. What is a skunk's favorite food?

Down

1. What is another thing that skunks like to eat?

2. Where do skunks live?

3. What does a skunk raise when it is getting ready to spray?

4. What should you do if a skunk raises its tail?

 Use details to describe your favorite animal.

Date: _____

Ricky loved to go camping. One day during reading class, he began to daydream about camping in the mountains. He thought about going fishing and riding horses. It would be fun to gather logs to build a campfire and cook hot dogs. He and his dad could set up the tent near some big trees. He wished he were in his canoe right now. Just then, Ricky heard his teacher say, "Ricky, it is your turn to read." Oh no! He had lost the place!

Circle these things from the story hidden in the picture below: a fish, a fishing pole, a log for the campfire, a hot dog, a tree and a canoe.

1. Where was Ricky during this story? _____

   _____

2. Where would Ricky like to have been? _____

   _____

Date: _____

Kelly is going to spend the night with her grandmother. She will need to take her nightdress, a shirt and some shorts. Into the suitcase go her toothbrush, toothpaste and hairbrush. Grammy told her to bring a swimsuit in case it was warm enough to swim. Mom said to pack her favorite pillow and storybooks. Dad said, "Don't forget to take Grammy's sunglasses that she left here last week." Now Kelly is ready to go!

Color the things that Kelly packed in her suitcase.

 A compound word is a big word that is made up of two small words. For example, cow + boy = cowboy. Find nine compound words in this story and circle them.

Date: _____

➤ **Sequencing** *means putting the events in a story in the order they happened.*

Last summer I learned how to swim. First, the teacher told me to hold my breath. Then I learned to put my head under water. I practiced kicking my feet. While I held on to a float, I paddled around the pool. Next, I floated to my teacher with my arms straight out. Finally, I swam using both my arms and my legs. I did it! Swimming is fun! This summer, I want to learn to dive off the diving board.

Number the pictures in the order that they happened in the story.

Unscramble the letters to tell what the boy in the story wants to do next.

EALNR   OT   IVDE

___ ___ ___ ___ ___   ___ ___   ___ ___ ___ ___

Date: _____

1. **Read the story.**

    My mother gave me some seeds. I dug some holes in the garden.
    I planted the seeds.
    Each day I watered the seeds. I waited for a few weeks to go by. Soon some flowers
    began to grow.

2. **Read the sentences below. Rewrite them in the correct order.**

    Some flowers began to grow.
    I planted the seeds.
    My mother gave me some seeds.
    I watered the seeds.

    _____

1. _____

    _____

2. _____

    _____

3. _____

    _____

4. _____

Date: _____

1. Read the story.

Tomorrow I will go swimming. I will put
on my swimsuit. I will jump in the water to
get wet. Then I will dive off the
diving board. Grandma will fix lunch
for me. Mom will swim with me after lunch.

2. Read the sentences below. Rewrite them in the correct order.

Mom will swim with me.
I will put on my swimsuit.
Grandma will fix lunch for me.
I will jump in the water.

_____

1. _____

_____

2. _____

_____

3. _____

_____

4. _____

Date: _____

1. **Read the story.**

    Dad and I went fishing today. We woke up
    very early. We ate breakfast. We left the
    house after we ate. We went to the bait
    store. Dad bought some worms. We caught
    five fish. Mom was happy to cook them for us.

2. **Read the sentences below. Rewrite them
    in the correct order.**

    We ate breakfast.
    Dad bought some bait.
    We woke up early.
    Mom cooked our fish.

    _____
    -
1. _____

    _____
    -
2. _____

    _____
    -
3. _____

    _____
    -
4. _____

Use story details to make a guess about what will happen next.

Mia and Rosa were playing hospital. Mia was the patient and Rosa was the doctor. Rosa pretended to take Mia's temperature. "You have a fever," she said. "You will have to lie down." Mia climbed onto the top bunk bed. "You need to sleep," Dr Rosa said. Mia rolled over too far and fell off the top bunk. "O-o-o-h, my arm!" yelled Mia. Her mother came to look. It was broken!

What do you think happened next? Write your answer here.

_____

To find out if your answer is correct, finish the sentence below by coloring only the spaces that have a dot in them.

Mia had to go to

Date: _____

One day, Sam was riding his bike to the baseball game. He had to be on time. He was the pitcher. Just ahead, Sam saw a little boy who had fallen off his bike. His knee was bleeding and he was crying. Sam asked him if he was okay, but the boy couldn't speak English. Sam knew the boy needed help getting home. If he stopped to help, he might be late for the game. Sam thought about it. He knew he had to do the right thing.

What do you think Sam did next? There are two paths through the maze. Draw a line down the path that shows what you think Sam did next.

What sentence from the story gives you a hint about what Sam decided to do? Write that sentence below.

_____

Date: _____

 Picturing a story can help the reader understand it better.

An artist drew the pictures that are in this book. Now it is your turn to be the artist! Read each sentence very carefully. Draw exactly what you read about in the sentence.

1. The green and yellow striped snake wiggled past the ants.

2. Wildflowers grew along the banks of the winding river.

3. On her sixth birthday, Shannon hung streamers and balloons on the walls.

Date: _____

Big, black clouds appeared in the sky. Lightning struck the tallest tree. The scared cow cried, "Moo!" It rained hard. Soon there was a mud puddle by the barn door. Hay blew out of the barn window.

Read the story above. Then go back and read each sentence again. Add to the picture everything that the sentences describe.

Date: _____

 Grouping like things together makes it easier to remember what you read.

Mom says, "Let's go out for ice cream! Clean your room, and then we will go." Your room is a mess. You need to put the blocks in the basket. The crayons must go in their box. The books must go on the shelf, and the marbles go in the jar. You can do it. Just think about that hot fudge sundae!

Draw a line from each item on the floor to the place it belongs. Color the things that you could use in school red. Color the toys blue.

Circle the food that does not belong in an ice cream store.

Look for similarities when grouping items.

Read the words in the Word Box. Write each word in the place where you would find these things at the mall.

Word Box

tickets	sandals	high heels	beans	big screen
tulip bulbs	peppers	fertilizer	popcorn	gardening gloves
sneakers	burritos	boots	pots	candy	tacos

1. **Sandie's Shoe Store**

2. **Movie Town Cinema**

3. **PEPE'S MEXICAN FOOD**

4. **Gale's Gardening Goodies**

Date: _____

Eating good food helps you grow up to be strong and healthy. There are many kinds of foods. Fish, chicken and beef are meats. Dairy foods include milk, cheese and yogurt. What kinds of bread do you like? I like muffins, bagels and biscuits. Fruits and vegetables, such as carrots, corn and apples, are good for you. They are full of vitamins.

Look at the pictures of different foods below. Draw a line from each food to the category it belongs to.

| Meats | Dairy | Breads | Fruits and Vegetables |

Date: _____

Compare *means to look for things that are the same.*
Contrast *means to look for things that are different.*

To solve the riddles in each box, read the clues in the horse. Then write the letters in the blanks with the matching numbers.

What kind of food does a racehorse like to eat?

____ ____ ____ ____   ____ ____ ____ ____
  11   5   10   3   11   9   9   2

1. What letter is in LOG, but not in DOG?
2. What letter is in DIME, but not in TIME?
3. What letter is in BITE, but not in BIKE?
4. What letter is in WEST, but not in REST?
5. What letter is in FAN, but not in FUN?
6. What letter is in BOX, but not in FOX?
7. What letter is in CAR, but not in CAN?
8. What letter is in ME, but not in MY?
9. What letter is in SOCK, but not in SACK?
10. What letter is in SEE, but not in BEE?
11. What letter is in FULL, but not in PULL?

Where does a rose sleep at night?

____ ____ ____ ____ ____ ____   ____ ____ ____
  11   1   9   4   8   7   6   8   2

Date: _____

Holly and Polly are twins. They are in the first grade. They look just alike, but they are very different. Holly likes to play softball and soccer. She likes to wear her hair braided when she goes out to play. She wears sporty clothes. Recess is her favorite part of school. Polly likes to read books and paint pictures. Every day she wears a ribbon in her hair to match her dress. Her favorite thing about school is going to the library. She wants to be a teacher some day.

Look at the pictures of Holly and Polly. Their faces look alike. Circle the things in both pictures that are different from each other.

Draw two lines under the words that tell what Holly and Polly do that is the same.

They play sports.   They love to paint.   They are in the first grade.

Date: _____

Juan's dad and Ann's dad are soldiers. Juan's dad is a captain in the Navy. He sails on the ocean in a large ship. Ann's dad is a pilot in the Air Force. He flies a jet. Juan and Ann miss their dads when they are gone for a long time. They write them letters and send them pictures. It is a happy day when their dads come home!

Draw a ☺ in the column under the correct dad. Some sentences may describe both dads.

		Juan's dad	Ann's dad	Both dads
1.	He is a captain.			
2.	He works on a ship.			
3.	Sometimes he is gone for a long time.			
4.	He is a pilot.			
5.	His child writes to him.			
6.	He is in the Air Force.			
7.	He is in the Navy.			
8.	It is a happy time when he comes home.			
9.	He flies a jet.			
10.	He is a soldier.			

Date: _____

 When you use your own thoughts to answer the question "How could that have happened?" you are **drawing conclusions**.

I bought a fancy rug today. It was made of brightly colored yarn. I placed it on the floor in front of the TV and sat on it. All of a sudden, it lifted me up in the air! The rug and I flew around the house. Then out the door we went. High above the trees, we soared like an eagle. Finally, the rug took me home and we landed in my backyard.

How could that have happened? To find out, use your crayons to trace over each line. Use a different color on each line. Write the letter from that line in the box at the bottom of the rug.

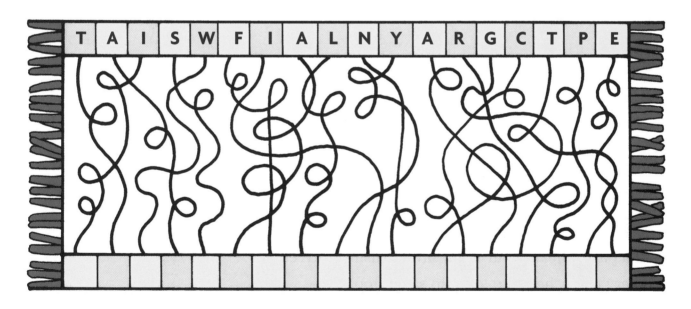

T A I S W F I A L N Y A R G C T P E

Could this story really happen? Draw a rug around your answer.

Yes   No

Date: _____

Have you ever heard a parrot talk? Parrots are able to copy sounds that they hear. You can train a parrot to repeat words, songs and whistles. But a parrot cannot say words that it has never heard. People can use words to make new sentences, but a parrot cannot.

Read each sentence. If it is true, color the parrot under True. If it is false, color the parrot under False.

	True	False
1. You could teach a parrot to sing "Happy Birthday."		
2. You could ask a parrot any question, and it could give the answer.		
3. A parrot could make up a fairy tale.		
4. If a parrot heard your mom say, "Brush your teeth," every night, he could learn to say it, too.		
5. It is possible for a parrot to repeat words in Spanish.		

Date: _____

 When you use what you know to make a decision, you are making an inference. Use details from the story to make decisions about the characters.

Circle the picture that answers the riddle.

1. I am a female. I like to watch movies and listen to music. My grandchildren love my oatmeal cookies. Who am I?

2. I live in the ocean. I swim around slowly, looking for something to eat. I have six more arms than you have. Who am I?

3. I am a large mammal. I live in the woods. I have fur. I stand up and growl when I am angry. Who am I?

4. I am an insect. If you touch me, I might bite you! I make tunnels under the ground. I love to come to your picnic! Who am I?

5. I have feathers. I also have wings, but I don't fly. I love to swim in icy water. Who am I?

Use story details to help you make decisions about the story.

James was the first boy in Miss Lane's class to find red spots on his face and arms. He scratched until his mom came to take him home. A week later, Amy and Jana got the spots. The next Monday, six more children were absent. Finally, everyone got well and came back to school. But this time, Miss Lane was absent. Guess what was wrong with her!

Color red spots on the correct answers.

1. What do you think was wrong with the children?

sore throats   chicken pox   broken arms

2. How do you know the spots were itchy?

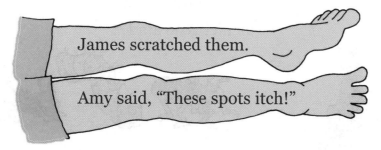

James scratched them.

Amy said, "These spots itch!"

3. How many children in all got sick?

2   5   9   4

4. Why do you think Miss Lane was absent? Write your answer.

_____

_____

Date: _____

Read the sentence below each picture. In the bubbles, write what each character could be saying.

Mr Giraffe asked Mr Zebra why he had stripes. Mr Zebra didn't know.

Mr Giraffe said that he should ask Mrs Owl. Mr Zebra agreed.

Mr Zebra asked Mrs Owl why he had stripes. Mrs Owl laughed.

Mrs Owl told Mr Zebra that the Magic Fairy had painted him that way!

Date: _____

 *In a story, there is usually a reason something happens. This is the **cause**. What happens as a result is the **effect**.*

Sandy went on a vacation in the mountains with her parents and little brother Austin. They were staying in a small cabin without any electricity or running water. It was fun to have lanterns at night and to bathe in the cold mountain stream. The biggest problem for Sandy was she missed her best friend, Kendra. Sandy found her dad's cell phone and called Kendra. They talked for nearly an hour! When Sandy's dad wanted to call his office, the cell phone was dead. He was NOT a happy camper!

Draw a line to match the first part of each sentence to the second part that makes it true.

1. Sandy used lanterns at night because

2. Sandy bathed in a stream because

3. Sandy felt better about missing Kendra because

4. Sandy's dad could not call his office because

she talked to her on the cell phone.

the cabin had no running water.

the cabin had no electricity.

the cell phone was dead.

It is important to follow the rules at school.

Read each rule below. Find the picture that shows what would happen if students did not follow that rule. Write the letter of the picture in the correct box.

1. You must walk, not run, in the halls.

2. Do not chew gum at school.

3. Come to school on time.

4. When the fire alarm rings, follow the leader outside.

5. Listen when the teacher is talking.

6. Keep your desk clean.

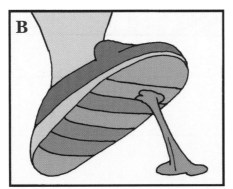

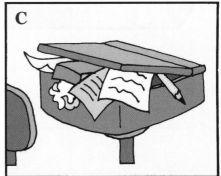

Date: _____

 *In a story, there is usually a reason something happens. This is the **cause**. What happens as a result is the **effect**.*

Wanda Wiggleworm was tired of living alone in the flowerpot, so she decided to enjoy herself. Last night, Wanda went to the Ugly Bug Ball. She looked her best, all slick and slimy. Carl Caterpillar asked her to dance. They twisted and wiggled around and around to the music. All of a sudden, they got tangled up. They tried to get free, but instead, they tied themselves in a knot! What would they do? They decided to get married and they lived happily ever after.

Unscramble each sentence about the story. Write the new sentence on the line.

1.

tangled	worms	when	got	danced.	they	The	up

_____

_____

2.

in	knot	They	married.	a	they	were	so	got	tied

_____

_____

Date: _____

 A character is a person or animal in a story. To help readers understand a character better, a story often gives details about the character.

Once upon a time there was a mixed-up queen named Margie. She got things mixed up. She wore her crown on her arm. She wore a shoe on her head. She painted every fingernail a different color. Then she painted her nose red! She used a fork to hold her hair in place. She wore a purple belt around her knees. The king didn't mind. He always wore his clothes backward!

Use the story and your crayons to help you follow these instructions:

1. Draw Margie's crown.

2. Draw her shoe.

3. Paint her fingernails and nose.

4. Draw what goes in her hair.

5. Draw her belt.

Circle the correct answer:

6. What makes you think Margie is mixed up?

   the way she dresses

   the way she talks

7. What makes you think the king is mixed up, too?

   He talks backward.

   He wears his clothes backward.

Date: _____

I love Miss Ticklefoot. She is my first-grade teacher.

To find out more about her, read each sentence below. Write a word from the Word Box in each blank that tells how she feels.

Word Box

sad	scared	silly	worried	happy	surprised

1. Miss Ticklefoot smiles when we know the answers.

_____

2. She is concerned when one of us is sick.

_____

3. She makes funny faces at us during recess.

_____

4. She cried when our fish died.

_____

5. She jumps when the fire alarm rings.

_____

6. Her mouth dropped open when we gave her a present!

_____

Date: _____

When Ty was four years old, he had two make-believe friends named Mr Go-Go and Mr Sasso. They lived in Ty's closet. When there was no one else around, Ty talked to Mr Go-Go while he played with his toys. Mr Go-Go was a good friend. He helped put Ty's toys away. Mr Sasso was not a good friend. Some days he forgot to make Ty's bed or brush Ty's teeth. One day he even talked back to Ty's mother. Another day Dad said, "Oh my! Who wrote on the wall?" Ty knew who did it ... Mr Sasso!

Read the phrase inside each crayon. If it describes Mr Go-Go, color it green. If it describes Mr Sasso, color it red. If it describes both, color it yellow.

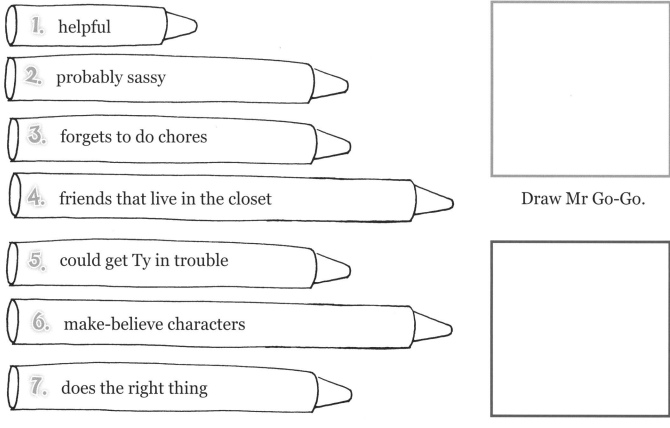

1. helpful

2. probably sassy

3. forgets to do chores

4. friends that live in the closet

Draw Mr Go-Go.

5. could get Ty in trouble

6. make-believe characters

7. does the right thing

Draw Mr Sasso.

Date: _____

Read the story and then answer the questions.

My Uncle's Airplane

My uncle has a new airplane. It is yellow with blue stripes.
The wings have stars on them. It flys high. He took me
on a trip in his new plane. The name of his plane is
Yellow Bird.

1. Who has a new airplane?

   _____

   -

   _____

2. What are the colors of the airplane?

   _____

   -

   _____

3. What are on the wings of the airplane?

   _____

   -

   _____

4. Who took a trip in the new plane?

   _____

   -

   _____

5. What is the name of the airplane?

   _____

   -

   _____

6. Does the airplane fly high or low?

   _____

   -

   _____

Read the story and then answer the questions.

If I Were King

I would like to be a king. I would wear a robe with diamonds on it. I would wear a gold crown on my head. I would call the land I rule "Funville." Every year we would have a parade. I would want all of the people in Funville to be happy.

1. What would I like to be?

   _____

   _____

2. What would be on my robe?

   _____

   _____

3. What would I wear on my head?

   _____

   _____

4. What would I call my land?

   _____

   _____

5. What would happen every year in Funville?

   _____

   _____

6. Do I want the people in Funville to be happy?

   _____

   _____

Date: _____

Read the story and then answer the questions.

Joel's Pets

Joel has three pets. He has two cats and one dog. Joel's cats are named Fifi and Foofoo. Joel's dog is named Hook. Joel gives his pets fresh food and water each day. He plays fetch with Hook.

1. How many pets does Joel have?

   _____

   _____

2. How many cats does Joel have?

   _____

   _____

3. How many dogs does Joel have?

   _____

   _____

4. What are the names of Joel's cats?

   _____

   _____

5. What is the name of Joel's dog?

   _____

   _____

6. What does Joel give to his pets?

   _____

   _____

Date: _____

Read the story and then answer the questions.

Larry the Frog

Larry is a frog. Larry is green with brown spots. He loves to play in the pond. Sometimes Larry catches flies. He likes to eat flies for dinner. After Larry catches flies, he hops around the pond.

1. What is Larry?

   _____

   -

   _____

2. What color is Larry?

   _____

   -

   _____

3. Where does Larry love to play?

   _____

   -

   _____

4. What does Larry catch?

   _____

   -

   _____

5. What does Larry like to eat for dinner?

   _____

   -

   _____

6. What does Larry do after he catches flies?

   _____

   -

   _____

Date: _____

Read the story and then answer the questions.

Karen's Doll

Karen's favorite toy is her doll. The doll's name is Kathy. Kathy has blonde hair and wears a pink dress. Karen was three years old when she got her doll. Kathy sleeps on Karen's bed when Karen is at school.

1. What is Karen's favorite toy?

   _____

   -

   _____

2. What is the name of Karen's doll?

   _____

   -

   _____

3. What color is Kathy's hair?

   _____

   -

   _____

4. What color is Kathy's dress?

   _____

   -

   _____

5. What does Kathy do when Karen is at school?

   _____

   -

   _____

6. Is Kathy a real person?

   _____

   -

   _____

Date: _____

Read the story and then answer the questions.

Chris Likes Science

My name is Chris. I like to read. I like stories about stars and planets the best. The book I am reading now is about the sun. The book has many pictures. It has a picture of the sun on the cover. We will study the sun in science class next year.

1. What is my name?
_____

_____

2. What kind of books do I like?
_____

_____

3. What am I reading about now?
_____

_____

4. What does the book I am reading have a lot of?
_____

_____

5. What is on the cover of this book?
_____

_____

6. What will I study next year at school?
_____

_____

Date: _____

Read the story and then answer the questions.

Rainy Day

Roy likes to play in the rain. When it rains, he puts on his raincoat and boots. He goes outside. Roy splashes in the puddles. Roy must think that he is a duck. Sometimes Meyer plays in the rain with Roy.

1. What does Roy like to play in?

   _____
   -
   _____

2. What does Roy put on when it rains?

   _____
   -
   _____

3. Where does Roy go?

   _____
   -
   _____

4. What does Roy splash in?

   _____
   -
   _____

5. What must Roy think he is?

   _____
   -
   _____

6. Who plays in the rain with Roy sometimes?

   _____
   -
   _____

Date: _____

Read the story and then answer the questions.

Rowe's Dog

My friend Rowe has a dog. I really like Rowe's dog. His dog is brown. She wears a red collar. Rowe plays with the dog a lot. Rowe's dog loves to chew on bones. I wish I had a dog like Rowe's.

1. What does my friend Rowe have?

   _____

   _____

2. Do I like Rowe's dog?

   _____

   _____

3. What color is Rowe's dog?

   _____

   _____

4. What color is the dog's collar?

   _____

   _____

5. What does Rowe's dog chew on?

   _____

   _____

6. What do I wish?

   _____

   _____

Date: _____

Read the story and then answer the questions.

Baby Chickens

A mother chicken sat on her nest. She was a big chicken with yellow feathers. She was sitting on some eggs. One day the eggs cracked open. Then some little chicks popped out of the eggs. Now the chicken had six chicks.

1. Where did the mother chicken sit?

   _____
   -
   _____

2. What color were her feathers?

   _____
   -
   _____

3. What was the mother chicken sitting on?

   _____
   -
   _____

4. What happened to the eggs one day?

   _____
   -
   _____

5. What came out of the eggs?

   _____
   -
   _____

6. How many chicks were there?

   _____
   -
   _____

Date: _____

Read the story and then answer the questions.

Wally the Whale

Wally is a big blue whale. Wally lives in the ocean. He swims with his whale friends. Sometimes Wally dives deep then he jumps high into the air. When he lands in the water, Wally makes a big splash.

1. What kind of animal is Wally?

_____

- -

_____

2. What color is Wally?

_____

- -

_____

3. Where does Wally live?

_____

- -

_____

4. Who does Wally swim with?

_____

- -

_____

5. What does Wally do after he dives deep?

_____

- -

_____

6. What happens when Wally lands in the water?

_____

- -

_____

Fill in the bubble next to the sentence that tells about each picture.

Example

○ **A**   A girl sits.   ○ **C**   A girl runs.

○ **B**   A girl walks.   ○ **D**   A girl eats.

1.

○ **A**   The boy plays ball.

○ **B**   The cat plays.

○ **C**   The girls run and play.

○ **D**   The cat runs.

2.

○ **A**   The book is on the desk.

○ **B**   He has two books.

○ **C**   The pen is next to the book.

○ **D**   The book is on the chair.

3.

○ **A**   We have a big bag.

○ **B**   She has a rabbit.

○ **C**   He has a rug and a pan.

○ **D**   She has a cat.

4.

○ **A**   Six donkeys sit.

○ **B**   The dog sits on a hill.

○ **C**   A goat plays in the mud.

○ **D**   A cat climbs a tree.

Read the story then answer each question. Fill in the bubble next to the best answer.

Pam has a dog. His name is Rags.
Rags likes to play.
Rags likes to run.
Rags likes to jump.
Rags is a good dog!

5. What kind of pet does Pam have?

○ **A**   cat

○ **B**   dog

○ **C**   rabbit

○ **D**   gerbil

6. What is a good title (name) for this story?

○ **A**   Rags the Dog

○ **B**   Frogs Jump

○ **C**   Apples Grow on Trees

○ **D**   Pam has a Bad Dog

7. What does Rags like to do?

○ **A**   skip

○ **B**   play

○ **C**   sing

○ **D**   eat

Fill in the bubble next to the correct answer.

8. What letter is in PAT, but not CAT?

○ **A**   P

○ **B**   C

○ **C**   A

○ **D**   T

9. Fill in the bubble next to the event that comes first.

○ **A**   Sue eats a piece of cake.

○ **B**   Mom opens the cake mix.

○ **C**   Sue adds eggs and milk to the mix.

○ **D**   Mom puts the mix in a bowl.

10. Fill in the bubble that answers the riddle.

I am an insect.

I bite people.

People don't like me.

I leave red marks on people.

Who am I?

○ **A**   a slug

○ **B**   a mosquito

○ **C**   a ladybug

○ **D**   a grasshopper

Answer Key

Phonics and Spelling

Page 6
1. goat   2. bike   3. cup
4. six   5. fire

Page 7
1. sub, s, b   2. pit, p, t   3. net, n, t
4. lap, l, p   5. top, t, p   6. sag, s, g

Page 8
Review that directions have been followed and matching lines have been drawn.

Page 9
Review that beginning k, w and r have sleepy eyes above and remaining letters are colored.

Page 10
Circle: gg, mm, nn, bb, ll, ll, tt, mm, nn, dd, pp;
3, 2, 4, 1

Page 11
hand: sand, land, band
ball: hall, call, mall, tall, wall, fall
dog: fog, jog, log, hog
cat: pat, sat, rat, mat, fat, hat, bat

Page 12
1. hill, crown   2. fiddle, spoon
3. clock   4. snow

Page 13
Color: spear, spoon, sponge, spill, spur, spaghetti, spaceship, spider
Cross: bike, airplane, lamp, hat, horse, compass; spinach

Page 14
Color: sneaker, snowflake, snowman, snorkel, snap, snail, sneeze, snout

Page 15
1. smoke   2. smile   3. smell

Page 16
1. stamp   2. stork   3. starfish
4. stapler   5. stick   6. stove

Page 17
1. Twirl!   2. Twelve   3. Twister
4. Tweezers 5. Tweet! Tweet!
6. Twenty

Page 18
red: 1, 2, 3, 4, 5, 6, 9, 11;
yellow: 7, 8, 10, 12

Page 19
1. th   2. ch   3. wh

Page 20
A. begin with th: the, this, then, that; end with th: bath, with
B. 1. bath   2. then   3. that
4. the   5. with   6. this

Page 21
A. begin with sh: ship, she, shape; end with sh: fish, wish, brush
B. 1. ship   2. shape   3. she
4. fish   5. brush   6. wish

Page 22
A. begin with ch: chin, chop; begin with wh: whale, when, which; end with ch: inch, which
B. 1. whale   2. chop   3. inch
4. which   5. when   6. chin

Page 23
A. a: pack, back; e: neck; i: stick; o: rock; u: duck
B. 1. neck   2. duck   3. stick
4. rock   5. pack   6. back

Page 24
A. ar: hard, part, farm; other words: are, star, jar
B. 1. hard   2. part   3. farm
4. are, star, jar

Page 25
A. 2–3 letter: or, for; 4–5 letter: corn, porch, horn, short
B. 1. short   2. porch   3. corn
4. horn   5. or   6. for

Page 26
Review that directions have been followed.

Page 27–30
1. A   2. B   3. B   4. C
5. C   6. B   7. B   8. B
9. B   10. A   11. B   12. C

Reading Skills

Page 32
1. a good reader
2. looks at the pictures
3. the title
4. the words

Page 33
Clowns can do funny tricks.

Page 34
Trucks do important work.
Dump truck, cement truck, fire truck, tank truck, flatbed truck

Page 35
A. KATE
B. 1. brave   2. friend   3. princess

Page 36

Across	Down
2. white	1. mice
5. bugs	2. woods
	3. tail
	4. run

Page 37

1. reading class
2. camping in the mountains

Page 38
Color: nightdress, shirt, shorts, toothbrush, toothpaste, hairbrush, swimsuit, pillow, storybooks, sunglasses

Page 39
6, 4, 2, 3, 1, 5
LEARN TO DIVE

Page 40
1. My mother gave me some seeds.
2. I planted the seeds.
3. I watered the seeds.
4. Some flowers began to grow.

Page 41
1. I will put on my swimsuit.
2. I will jump in the water.
3. Grandma will fix lunch for me.
4. Mom will swim with me.

Page 42
1. We woke up early.
2. We ate breakfast.
3. Dad bought some bait.
4. Mom cooked our fish.

Page 43
Review the prediction;
Mia had to go to a real hospital.

Page 44
Review the prediction;
He knew he had to do the right thing.

Page 45–46
Review that directions have been followed.

Page 47
Review lines and coloring;
red: books, crayons; blue: blocks, marbles;
sandwich

Page 48
1. sandals, high heels, sneakers, boots
2. tickets, big screen, popcorn, candy
3. beans, peppers, burritos, tacos
4. tulip bulbs, fertilizer, gardening gloves, pots

Page 49
meats: fish, chicken, roast
dairy: yoghurt, milk, cheese
breads: bagels, muffins, biscuits
fruits and vegetables: carrots, corn, apple

Page 50
fast food;
1. L   2. D   3. T   4. W
5. A   6. B   7. R   8. E
9. O   10. S   11. F
flower bed;

Page 51
Circle: hair, clothes, socks, shoes, bat/ball, paintbrush/book;
They are in the first grade.

Page 52
1. Juan's dad   2. Juan's dad
3. both dads   4. Ann's dad
5. both dads   6. Ann's dad
7. Juan's dad   8. both dads
9. Ann's dad   10. both dads

Page 53
It was a flying carpet. Review that directions have been followed.

Page 54
1. True   2. False   3. False
4. True   5. True

Page 55
1. grandmother   2. octopus
3. bear   4. ant
5. penguin

Page 56
1. chicken pox
2. James scratched them.
3. 9
4. She got chicken pox, too.

Page 57
1. Giraffe: Why do you have stripes?
   Zebra: I don't know.
2. Giraffe: You should ask Mrs Owl.
   Zebra: Yes.
3. Zebra: Why do I have stripes?
   Owl: Ha Ha Ha.
4. Owl: The Magic Fairy painted you that way!

Page 58
1. the cabin had no electricity.
2. the cabin had no running water.
3. she talked to her on the cell phone.
4. the cell phone was dead.

Page 59
1. E   2. B   3. D   4. F
5. A   6. C

Page 60
1. The worms got tangled up when they danced. 2. They were tied in a knot so they got married.

Page 61
1–5. Review that directions have been followed.
6. the way she dresses
7. He wears his clothes backward.

Page 62
1. happy   2. worried   3. silly
4. sad   5. scared   6. surprised

Page 63
1. green   2. red   3. red   4. yellow
5. red   6. yellow   7. green

Page 64
1. uncle   2. yellow and blue
3. stars   4. me/the author
5. Yellow Bird   6. high

Page 65
1. king   2. diamonds
3. gold crown   4. Funville
5. a parade   6. yes

Page 66
1. three   2. two   3. one
4. Fifi and Foofoo   5. Hook
6. fresh food and water

Page 67
1. a frog
2. green with brown spots
3. in the pond   4. flies   5. flies
6. He hops around the pond.

Page 68
1. her doll   2. Kathy   3. blond
4. pink   5. sleeps on Karen's bed
6. no

Page 69
1. Chris
2. stories about stars and planets
3. the sun
4. pictures
5. a picture of the sun
6. the sun

Page 70
1. the rain   2. raincoat and boots
3. outside   4. puddles   5. a duck
6. Meyer

Page 71
1. a dog   2. yes   3. brown   4. red
5. bones   6. to have a dog like Rowe's

Page 72
1. on her nest   2. yellow   3. eggs
4. they cracked open   5. chicks
6. six

Page 73
1. a whale
2. blue
3. in the ocean
4. his whale friends
5. he jumps high into the air
6. he makes a big splash

Page 74–76
1. B   2. A   3. B   4. B
5. B   6. A   7. B   8. A
9. B   10. B

SCHOLASTIC Learning Express

Congratulations!

I, _____

am a Scholastic Superstar!

Paste a photo or draw a
picture of yourself.

I have completed Phonics and Reading Skills L1.

Presented on _____